How to Earn at Least $100,000 a Year In Network Marketing

Study Guide

by

RANDY GAGE

Entire Contents © 2001
Prime Concepts Group, Inc.
www.NetworkMarketingTimes.com

Second Edition

Introduction

Congratulations! By choosing network marketing, either as a supplemental business, or a new career, you have shown yourself to be a leader. Someone who isn't happy with mediocrity and the status quo ... someone who knows there is a better way. You've just discovered it. Congratulations and welcome. You've joined an industry with over 12 million distributors around the world who will do in the neighborhood of 60 to 70 billion dollars this year. As predicted more than a decade ago — networking has truly emerged as the new paradigm of personal and business development for the nineties. The purpose of this Study Guide is to get you started in the easiest, most effective manner possible. You'll avoid some of the common pitfalls and discover some things that will accelerate your journey to success in your networking business.

This Study Guide is divided into 12 sections — each one corresponding to a segment in the *How to Earn at Least $100,000 a Year in Network Marketing* audiotape album. If you follow along with the tapes — writing in the book as you go — you'll get the most out of both resources and achieve the maximum retention. If you don't have the tapes, you'll find the correct answers located in the back of the Study Guide.

Section One and Two are the "What You Need to Know First" and "Getting Started" training which, ideally, should be done with your sponsor. This meeting will help your sponsor understand what you hope to achieve in your business, and provide you the chance to develop a close working relationship with them. Afterward, you can replay the "Getting Started" tape as many times as necessary so you can duplicate this process with those you sponsor.

From there, you'll learn recruiting methods, sponsoring techniques and business-building strategies that will take your business to the level you want to go. This album and Study Guide are the result of my 15+ years in the industry, my experience working with MLM companies around the world, and coaching thousands of individual distributors. These techniques are not abstract theories or things I read in books — they are the result of real world experience. If you learn these techniques — and assiduously apply them — you can earn <u>at least</u> $100,000 a year in your network marketing business.

Please take your business seriously. Just because you haven't invested hundreds of thousands of dollars into your business doesn't mean that you can't earn an income greater than that of many of the top entrepreneurs in this country. If you run your business like a hobby — you'll get a hobby income. Run it like a business and you'll earn a big business income.

Don't talk to anyone about your new business yet!

The time for that will come soon. However, your sponsor is committed to helping you with your first presentations. It's better if you don't try to explain your new business until after you have some training and help from your sponsorship line. For now, just write the name and phone number of anyone you want to talk to in the space provided in this booklet.

There are several things necessary for success in network marketing. But of greater interest are some of the things people think they need — but actually don't. Here are some of the things you may believe are necessary for your success — but actually prevent you from reaching it:

The 5 things you don't need to be successful in Network Marketing ...

1. Credentials or Degrees

Thousands of people have been successful in networking without the benefit of college degrees and the like. Personally, I'm a high school dropout. Since networking is so unlike other businesses, the rules are different here. It's quite possible, actually quite common, to build a large successful organization without having any credentials or degrees. An argument could almost be made against having diplomas in this business, for people may feel that because their sponsor has an advanced business degree — they need one too. This is unduplicatable and entirely unnecessary. If you or your sponsor has a degree, great. It's just not necessary for success in network marketing.

2. Approval

Of anyone, except yourself. Sometimes even your spouse may not approve of your networking business. This is actually a frequent initial response, but we've seen thousands of people who have built huge businesses without the help of their spouse. Of course, after that, the spouse usually comes on board enthusiastically and things really take off.

One of the hardest facts of business to face is that not everybody is ready for success, nor is as enlightened as you. Don't be at all surprised to find that some of your closest friends and family members will ridicule you; not join your organization and/or even listen to a presentation; question your sanity; ask why someone with a "real" job would "mess around with one of those multi-level deals"; or all of the above. Then they will feel obligated to regale you with horror stories of people who "got a horrible rash just drinking that stuff," or have "a garage full of that stuff they can't get rid of." It's best to give these "well-meaning" souls a wry smile, thank them for their input and get away from them as quickly as possible.

3. Friends & Family in Your Network

Now please don't misunderstand; if you get them in your group, great! I know families with three generations in their networking business and it's a beautiful thing to behold. Other times, the hardest presentation you ever give might be to your sister or best friend. Sometimes you just can't be a prophet in your own hometown. Networking is full of individuals who have built networks in the thousands without having a single member of their family, or so-called best friends, in their group. I know, because I'm one of them.

4. Cheap Advice

Oftentimes a new distributor will get involved with network marketing and get all kinds of well-meaning advice from friends who have never built a networking business. If you want to know how to fly airplanes, you must get advice from an expert pilot. If you want to build a network, look at your sponsorship line and find someone who has already built a large network. Those are the people to seek out for advice.

5. Perfection

The perfect company, product line, or compensation plan hasn't been invented yet. Like everything in nature, it must evolve. Your job is to look at the whole picture — and if the pluses outweigh the minuses — get started. If you sit around waiting for perfection — you'll be waiting forever. Don't make the mistake many novices make — which is to think that they can't do anything until they have tried every single product, read every scrap of literature and completely understood every minute detail of the compensation plan. Having said that:

Here are 3 things you do need to be successful in Network Marketing ...

1. Desire

A desire to really do this and get out of the Rat Race forever. If you really understand this business and have a true desire to help yourself and others — you're already 90% there. Most people are happy with the way things are. People who desire better are the ones who change the world.

2. Enthusiasm

I can't begin to tell you how many times I have seen brand new distributors — with no training, no experience and no in-depth knowledge — go out and build a network of forty or sixty people their first month. They don't do this with skill, knowledge or technique — they just muscle it through with sheer, unadulterated enthusiasm. Approach this adventure with the excitement it deserves; don't attempt it, just jump in, roll up your sleeves, make up your mind and just do it!

3. Action

If you're waiting for the perfect plan — the perfect plan is <u>to take action</u>. You have to get started. Will you make mistakes? Of course you will! But, we're not brain surgeons here; nobody's going to die. Mistakes are part of the learning process and strengthen you for the long term. This Study Guide, the accompanying audiotape, and your sponsorship line will make sure you don't make any major mistakes which will harm your business, so relax and don't be afraid to move ahead. **Knowledge without action is only a potential for Power.** You've got the knowledge you need ... you've shown your wisdom by becoming a networker.

The purpose of this series is to help you **turn Knowledge into Action ... and Action into Achievement**. Network marketing has taken me from a lack consciousness to a prosperity one ... from self-doubt to self-assurance ... from poverty to a self-made millionaire. I owe my success to many people. In respect to the love, guidance and care they have shown me — I feel a responsibility to continue the process — and share this knowledge with you. Make the most of it. You deserve it!

Randy Gage
Miami Beach, Florida
May 2001

Notes:

What You Need to Know First

I. [   ]

II. [   ]

III. [   ]

IV. [   ]

V. [   ]

VI. Earn income two ways:

    1. Creating [   ]

    2. Creating [   ]

VII. [   ]

THE SEQUENCE

Step One — Qualifying Question

❏ **YES (Pre-Approach Packet)** ❏ No ⇨ Explore becoming a retail customer

⬇

Step Two — The Presentation

❏ **YES** ❏ Maybe ❏ No ⇨ Suggest becoming a product customer or find another prospect

⬇ ⬇

Step Three — The Follow-up Process

❏ **YES** ❏ Maybe ❏ No ⇨ Find another prospect

⬇ ⬇

Additional follow-up

Step Four — The Enrollment

❏ **YES**

⬇

"Get Started" Training

BUILDING YOUR SYSTEM:

Step	Action	Tools to Use
ONE	Ask Qualifying Questions	PRE-APPROACH PACKET: Lifestyle Freedom Pack Screening Tapes or Books
TWO	The Presentation	COMPANY MATERIALS PACKAGE: Product Catalog Business Plan Brochure Presentation Kit Product Sample(s) "Your Destiny" or "Future Choice" Book
THREE	The Follow-up Process	FOLLOW-UP PACKAGE: Product Tapes Company Profile Testimonial Type Audios Incentive Brochure
	Additional Follow-up Step	Company Video Publicity Reprints
FOUR	ENROLLMENT TOOLS: "First Steps" Booklet "Getting Started" Tape "Secrets of a Dynamic Day" Tape "The Greatest Networker in the World" Book "What You Need to Know First" Tape	

"You cannot sell your way to the top...

You cannot sponsor your way to the top...

You can only teach the system to make it to the top."

-R.G.

Notes:

Notes:

Notes:

Notes:

Getting Started

DO IT NOW!
(If You Have Not Already)

This is a list of things you should have already done by this point. Please check it to make sure you've completed all of these things. Then, move ahead to Section Two — Getting Started!

Place your first order.

You must use the products or services personally so you can get excited about them.

How much should you order? Somewhere between what you need — and where you're nervous. I say this only halfway in jest. You see, we've found that "just what you need" is not enough.

You'll need some inventory for reselling to new distributors, samples for temporarily out-of-stock items and personal marketing. You certainly don't want to have a garage or warehouse full of product. But do make sure you have enough product on hand to build your business.

Schedule your "Get Started" training with your sponsor.

Ideally, this should take place within 48 hours of the time you sponsor in.

Schedule between two and four hours for this training and follow along in Section Two of this Study Guide. Long distance, this can be done by phone.

Buy a Daily Planner or Appointment Book.

Bring this to your "Getting Started" training meeting.

Begin your Prospect List.

Remember, don't talk to anyone about your business yet. Do that only after you have finished the Get Started Training. For now, begin writing down the name and phone number of anyone you think of on page 2-8.

Review the 5 "Get Started" training tools you received from your sponsor.

a) Read *"The Greatest Networker in the World"* book.

b) Listen to the *"Secrets of a Dynamic Day"* tape. Set aside 15 minutes every morning to repeat this process.

c) Listen to the *"What You Need to Know First"* tape.

d) Listen to the *"Getting Started"* tape.

e) Work along in this booklet or the *"First Steps"* booklet.

Sign the Commitment Form on page 2-4.

Success does not come overnight; it takes work. We ask that you make a one-year commitment to your business. Accept the fact that there is a training period. Just like any job or occupation — networking takes training. It does not take years or cost thousands of dollars, but you do need to learn some new things. Of course, you will "earn as you learn," but it's still a good idea to consider your first six months a learning experience. For the average networker, working your business only 7 to 10 hours a week, a one-year commitment is a realistic approach. We believe that if you follow our duplicatable system for that time — you will be so pleased with the results that you will be networking for the rest of your life!

GET STARTED TRAINING
10 Steps to Success

❏ Set your goals.

❏ Schedule your appointment book.

❏ Learn the basic company procedures.

❏ Order your business cards.

❏ Open a business checking account or get a separate credit card for your business.

❏ Purchase the business-building materials you will need to get started.

❏ Study the core qualities of a network marketing leader.

❏ Complete your prospect list of at least 100 names.

❏ Get at least 10 "pre-approach" packets in circulation.

❏ Schedule your first presentations.

COMMITMENT FORM

I, _____, make the following commitments to myself in order to build a successful network marketing organization and ensure a secure future.

I will:

- devote at least 7 to 10 hours a week to my business,
- spend daily self-development time, and
- look upon my first 6 months as a learning experience.

I will build my business for at least one year, and then I will evaluate it accordingly. I recognize that the people I sponsor are my responsibility. My first responsibility is to become successful myself, and then duplicate this with my people. I will faithfully follow the system so my efforts can be duplicated.

_____   _____
Signed   Date

_____   _____
Witnessed by   Date

Make a copy of this page and give it to your sponsor.

GOALS

To be effective, goals must be specific, measurable and written down. Take a few minutes and write down what you would like to accomplish now. You may wish to seek some advice from your sponsor in this area.

I will reach 1,000 in group volume by_____.

The reason I started a network marketing business is

_____

_____

_____

_____

_____

_____

_____

At the end of my six-month training period, I would like to be earning $_____ a month.

My 2-to 4-year plan is

_____

_____

_____

_____

_____

_____

_____

Make a copy of this page and give it to your sponsor.

The goal of talking to people is not to sponsor them — it's to get an appointment for a presentation. Simply feel out the prospect to see if there is interest — to know if you have a qualified prospect.

If so — get the appointment.

We don't want to tell a prospect

until we can tell him

!

MEMORY JOGGERS

Whom Do You Know...
named Joe
who looks like Tom Cruise
who just quit smoking
who just moved away
in politics
at the United Way
that you met on a plane
who flies planes
in Radio/TV
who looks like Tina Turner
named Debbie
who needs extra money
at the gym

Who is Your...
Mail Carrier
Newspaper Carrier
Dentist
Minister/Rabbi/Priest
Florist
Lawyer
Insurance Agent
Accountant
Congressperson
Pharmacist
Veterinarian
Favorite Waiter/Waitress
Chiropractor
Butcher
Baker
Bank Officer
Printer
Optometrist/Ophthalmologist
Travel Agent
Hairstylist
Photographer
Architect
Exterminator
Dry Cleaner

Who is Your...
Mechanic
Landlord
Grocer
Carpet Cleaner

Who Sold You Your...
House/Condo
Computer
Carpet
Car
TV/Stereo
Wedding Rings
Glasses/Contact Lenses
Vacuum
Boat
Camper
Furniture
Air Conditioner
Appliances
Tupperware
Tires

Who Is Related to You...
Parents
Grandparents
Sisters
Brothers
Aunts
Uncles
Cousins

Who...
lives next door
lives down the block
lives across the street
lives upstairs/downstairs
teaches your children
was your best man/ushers

Who...
was your Maid of
    Honor/Bridesmaids
are your babysitter's parents
was a service buddy
did you go to school with
used to be your teachers/
    professors
is your old boss
fixes your TV
worked with you in past jobs
went with you to the beach
owns a restaurant
installed your appliances
is the President of the PTA
is in the local Chamber of
    Commerce
goes to church with you
watched the Super Bowl with
    you
is a policeman
is in the military
works at the video club
is an actor

Also...
Get out your holiday card
list, your address book and
any business cards you've
collected. If someone's name
is in there — they should be
on your list. Take out the
Yellow Pages and flip
through from A to Z to
refresh your memory.

1. _____
2. _____
3. _____
4. _____
5. _____
6. _____
7. _____
8. _____
9. _____
10. _____
11. _____
12. _____
13. _____
14. _____
15. _____
16. _____
17. _____
18. _____
19. _____
20. _____
21. _____
22. _____
23. _____
24. _____
25. _____

26. _____
27. _____
28. _____
29. _____
30. _____
31. _____
32. _____
33. _____
34. _____
35. _____
36. _____
37. _____
38. _____
39. _____
40. _____
41. _____
42. _____
43. _____
44. _____
45. _____
46. _____
47. _____
48. _____
49. _____
50. _____

51. _____
52. _____
53. _____
54. _____
55. _____
56. _____
57. _____
58. _____
59. _____
60. _____
61. _____
62. _____
63. _____
64. _____
65. _____
66. _____
67. _____
68. _____
69. _____
70. _____
71. _____
72. _____
73. _____
74. _____
75. _____

76. _____
77. _____
78. _____
79. _____
80. _____
81. _____
82. _____
83. _____
84. _____
85. _____
86. _____
87. _____
88. _____
89. _____
90. _____
91. _____
92. _____
93. _____
94. _____
95. _____
96. _____
97. _____
98. _____
99. _____
100. _____

101. _____
102. _____
103. _____
104. _____
105. _____
106. _____
107. _____
108. _____
109. _____
110. _____
111. _____
112. _____
113. _____
114. _____
115. _____
116. _____
117. _____
118. _____
119. _____
120. _____
121. _____
122. _____
123. _____
124. _____
125. _____

126. _____
127. _____
128. _____
129. _____
130. _____
131. _____
132. _____
133. _____
134. _____
135. _____
136. _____
137. _____
138. _____
139. _____
140. _____
141. _____
142. _____
143. _____
144. _____
145. _____
146. _____
147. _____
148. _____
149. _____
150. _____

Notes:

Notes:

Notes:

Notes:

"Survival Training"

HOW TO SURVIVE 90 DAYS WITH NO MONEY

I. The Realities of the Business

II. How to Work Smart

III. Handling Objections

IV. The Essence of the Business

V. Organization

VI. Duplication

REALITIES OF THE BUSINESS

The mind set to create:

PERSEVERING IN THE BUSINESS

"The only people who lose in network marketing are the people who quit too soon."

■ Story of someone in your company and the people who dropped out above them.

I. THE REALITIES OF THE BUSINESS
(a/k/a How to Defeat the Forces of Evil)

■ No shows

■ Drop-outs

■ MLM junkies

■ People with no dreams

■ Alligators

II. HOW TO WORK SMART

■ Using tools instead of you

■ Putting your sponsorship line to work for you

■ Utilizing the meetings

■ Fax-on-demands, demand conferences, conference calls, etc.

■ Adhering to the system

III. HANDLING OBJECTIONS

- ■ Accept the objection

- ■ Answer opinions with facts

- ■ "Feel," "Felt," "Found"

- ■ Most objections are actually questions

- ■ Prospects with lots of objections are usually quite interested

IV. THE ESSENCE OF THE BUSINESS

1.

2.

3.

Must be done simultaneously.

The three areas to work on:

- ■ Self-Development

- ■ Products

- ■ Business-Building

V. ORGANIZATION
(Lack of organization is a major cause of dropouts.)

- ■ Planner or appointment book

- ■ Lead follow-through system

- ■ Designated work area and desk

- ■ Scheduling their hours each week

- ■ File by line

Required Reading:

"The Seven Habits of Highly Effective People," by Stephen Covey.

VI. DUPLICATION

- Make sure they understand the system

- How to be independent

- Reinforce why the system is important

Notes:

Notes:

Notes:

Notes:

How to Talk to People

The goal of talking to people is not to sponsor them — it's to get an appointment for a presentation. Simply feel out the prospect to see if there is interest — to know if you have a qualified prospect.

If so — get the appointment.

We don't want to tell a prospect [   ]

until we can tell him [   ]!

The Process:

□□□□□□

□□□□□□

□□□□□□ OR □□□□□□

□□□□□□ OR □□□□□□

Sales Types	vs.	Non-Sales Types
10%		90%
No Fear		Fear of Rejection
Not duplicatable		Very duplicatable

Where do you see the best potential to build your business?

Qualifying Questions:

■ "Do you like your job?"

■ "Have you ever thought about opening your own home-based business?"

■ "Have you ever thought about developing a second income?"

■ "Do you make what you're worth?"

■ "I'm in marketing ... ," "I'm in the marketing business ...," "I own my own marketing business ..."

■ "I'm involved in a new venture that you may be interested in. You'd be your own boss; there's unlimited income potential and it's residual income. I have some materials you can review to see if it's right for you..."

■ "I've got a business that may be perfect for you. You'd be your own boss; there's unlimited income potential and it's residual income. I have some materials you can review to see if it's right for you..."

■ "You consider yourself open-minded don't you? I'm involved in a marketing business and I'm looking for a couple of key people who want to make money on the side. I'd love to run it by you."

■ "I'm involved in a marketing business with some large profit potential. I thought I'd call to see if you're interested in making some money on the side. Are you in the market for more money, more time or both?"

■ "I have a large volume marketing business ..."

OR

■ "I've recently started working with some people who have a large volume marketing business ... "

" ... and it's really hot right now. It just so happens we're expanding in (City) and we're in the process of talking to a couple of key people. You impress me as someone who's looking for more out of life. If you're really interested, I might find some time to show it to you."

■ "I'll help you make the calls or you can make the calls."

"Jesse, I'm working with a guy (gal) who makes a lot of money in marketing. He's looking for another person or two and I gave him your name. I can't tell you anything about it, but his name is Jeff Smith and he's going to be calling you ..."

"What's it about?"

"Jesse, I don't understand it all, so I can't really explain it. Jeff can explain it — he's a specialist in this area — and he's really good ..."

"Can't you tell me anything?"

"Yeah, it's really good and you can make a lot of money. Jeff is one of the top people in the marketing industry. He's sharp and he knows how to make money."

Jeff:
"Hi Jesse, this is Jeff Smith. Mary Morales tells me we need to talk (get together)."

The Pre-Approach Packet:

■ Screens out the prospects from the suspects.

■ Is designed to get an appointment with prospects...and disqualify the non-prospects.

■ Works best if loaned out with a sense of urgency (24-48 hours).

■ Lets you give presentations only to pre-sold prospects.

■ Reverses the dynamics of the sponsoring process.

■ Protects you and your non-sales types from unnecessary rejection.

■ Makes you more duplicatable.

Recommended Pre-Approach Pack:

■ **Lifestyle Freedom Pack**
(*Money for Life* Special Report and *Escape the Rat Race* audiotape in specially-designed album).

Alternate Choices
(Mix & Match)

■ **Tapes**
- *"Escape the Rat Race"*
- *"Future Choice/Rat Race Audio Album"*

■ **Booklets**
- *"Money, Money, Money, Money, Money"*
- *"Money for Life"* Special Report
- *"Are You Walking Past A Fortune?"*

■ **Books**
- *"Your Destiny: Your Life & Work Become One"*
- *"Future Choice: Why Network Marketing May Be Your Best Career Choice"*
- *"The Greatest Opportunity in the History of the World"*

Using A Pre-Approach Pack:

The purpose of a pre-approach packet is to separate the prospects from the suspects. In real terms, it's meant to disqualify the non-prospects and lead prospects to an appointment.

I recommend that you have 10 pre-approach packets — and keep them in constant circulation. They make you no money sitting at home. Keep them circulating and they can make you wealthy. Get one back from Jim, give it to Shawn, get it back from Shawn, give it to Sherry, etc.

If your company has no pre-approach packet, I have developed a generic one called the Lifestyle Freedom Pack, which I recommend. This packet is a special album holding a copy of the *"Escape the Rat Race"* audiotape and the *"Money for Life"* Special Report.

Here's how using a pre-approach packet works: When you meet or are speaking to a potential prospect, ask them a qualifying question:

■ "Have you ever thought about opening your own home-based business?"

■ "Would you be interested in developing a second income?"

■ "Do you like your job?"

■ "Are you making what you're really worth?"

(Look for more detailed examples on pages 4-4 through 4-6)

People who don't respond positively are not business-builder prospects. See if they have an interest in your product line and, if so, give them that information.

People who respond favorably should be moved into the system, starting with a pre-approach packet. This packet is your first chance to create a business-like impression with your prospect.

We say always that we're "looking for people who are looking." We want to find people with dreams or people that we can help rediscover their dreams. Then we need to know if they are willing to work to achieve those dreams. Finally, we must know that they are open-minded and willing to consider an unconventional business like network marketing. The pre-approach packet lets us know if we have such a person.

When a prospect responds to your initial question in a positive way — it's usually with some reservations or questions. It's not unusual to get replies like:

■ "Maybe. It depends on what it is,"

■ "Yes, depending on what it was," or

■ "It sounds interesting, but I would have to know more about it."

This is exactly the kind of reply you are looking for. It's not realistic to expect people to blurt out: "Sounds great, sign me up!"

You wouldn't want such people if they did. Someone who shows some interest, but has some guarded skepticism is exactly what you want. Those are the people to give your packet to.

The important part of this process is to create a sense of urgency. Let your prospect know that other prospects are waiting for this material and that they may preview it for 48 hours only. Get their commitment that they will review it in that time.

If they balk at 48 hours — saying, for example, that they can't get to it for 4 days — tell them that you have other people to review it in the meantime and you will bring it back in four days. Don't just say it, mean it. Keep your packets in constant circulation.

When you return after 48 hours to collect your packet, ask your prospect simply:

■ "Well, what do you think?"

Their answer should fall into one of three categories:

1) "That looks very interesting, but it's not something I'm interested in ..."

2) "I'm not interested in that pyramid stuff. My brother-in-law has a garage full of water filters, blah, blah, blah!!"

3) "Wow! Sounds intriguing. But what's the company, it doesn't say what the products are ..."

People who respond like the #1 example simply are not people who are looking. They did not catch the vision and are best handled by offering them information about your products. See if you can interest them in becoming a direct or retail customer.

The people who respond in the second manner are closed-minded people who don't want to be confused by the facts. If you're using my Lifestyle Freedom Pack, it's obvious they didn't even read the Special Report. You can argue with this type of person, but I don't recommend it.

I suggest you get back your materials and get away from them as quickly as possible.

The "Wow" replies are the keepers. These are the people you want to move to step two, which is actually giving them a presentation.

If it's possible, do it right then. If not, schedule a specific time and place for this to happen. If you've been using the pre-approach pack long distance, do a presentation on the phone and send out your company materials packet.

By using a pre-approach in this way, you'll get the most results from the limited amount of time you have to work your business. You'll only be making presentations to qualified prospects and you'll dramatically reduce the rejection that you and your people will face.

Notes:

Notes:

Notes:

Notes:

Secrets of Successful Presentations

To have a successful presentation, you must first get a prospect's

.

To do this, you must lead with the

and substantiate it with the

.

People don't buy

;

they don't buy

;

they buy the

they expect to receive from these things.

Features	vs.	Benefits
are about:		**are about:**
• You		• The Prospect
• Your Products		
• Your Company		
• Network Marketing		

If you can put the words "You get..." in front of a statement, it's probably a benefit. If not, it's probably a feature. Another great way to convert features into benefits is to ask the question "Which means?"

Required reading:
Cash Copy by Dr. Jeffrey Lant.

STEP ONE:

[   ]

■ Unlimited Income Potential

■ Choose the People you work with

■ Tax Advantages

■ Travel Opportunities

■ Empowering Others

■ Personal Growth

■ Minimal Start-up Costs

This is the Dream-Building Stage!

STEP TWO:

```

```

■ Show how your compensation plan works.

■ Show how networking works (3x3's or 5x5's).

■ Don't assault the prospect with every nuance of the compensation plan.

Note: It's important to make the connection that network marketing is the only method to achieve the incentives you just discussed.

STEP THREE:

■ Training Materials

■ Seminars, Conventions and other support events

■ Collateral Sales & Sponsoring Materials

■ Customer Service Department

■ Credibility

■ Security

STEP FOUR:

- ■ Product <u>benefits</u> foremost.

- ■ Overview of product lines.

- ■ Relate your testimonial and talk about your favorite product or two.

- ■ If you have a product demonstration, this is the time to do it.

STEP FIVE:

■ Make a Choice — Interested or Not

■ Make a Choice — Business-Builder or Customer

If the prospects are not interested — thank them for their time and move on to another prospect.

If the prospects want to be a customer — sell them their first product order.

If the prospects are interested in becoming a business builder, but not decided — move them to the follow-up step.

If the prospects are ready to be a business-builder — sell them their first order, enroll them, give them their materials and schedule their "Get Started" training.

Offer the 3 options:

1. Small Business

2. Big Business

3. Shop by Phone, Shop at Home or Preferred Customer Plan, etc.

I ncentives

N etwork Marketing

C ompany

O ur Products

M aking A Choice

E nrollment

Don't pre-judge for people. Don't assume they aren't interested in the business. Present the entire picture, and then let the prospect decide what is right for him or her.

Don't ☐☐☐☐☐☐☐☐☐☐☐☐☐☐☐ people …

☐☐☐☐☐☐☐☐☐☐☐☐☐☐☐ them!

■ Following a standardized presentation gives your group the chance to duplicate you.

■ Explore the possibilities of creating a presentation kit if your company does not provide one.

■ Use materials that are congruent with your opportunity — brochures from printing presses, not copy machines. No knock-off audio or videotapes — first-class professional materials only.

BUILDING YOUR SYSTEM:

Step	**Action**	**Tools to Use**
ONE	Ask Qualifying Questions	Pre-Approach Pack _____ _____ _____
TWO	The Presentation	Company Materials Package _____ _____ _____ _____ _____
THREE	The Follow-Up Process	Follow-Up Package _____ _____ _____ _____
	Additional Follow-Up	_____ _____
FOUR	Enrollment	

"How to Earn at Least $100,000 a Year in Network Marketing" Study Guide
"What You Need to Know First" Tape
"Getting Started" Tape
"Secrets of a Dynamic Day" Tape
"The Greatest Networker in the World" Book

Notes:

Notes:

Notes:

Notes:

Conducting Powerful, Effective Meetings

The purpose of a meeting is

┌───┐
│   │
└───┘.

A meeting is judged a success, <u>not</u> by whether product or a distributor kit was sold — but by whether another meeting was scheduled!

CONDUCTING POWERFUL, EFFECTIVE MEETINGS

Meetings should be:

- Fast-paced

- Intriguing

- Informational

- Professional

- FUN!

NOT ALL MEETINGS ARE IN HOTELS!

- Demand conferences

- Conference calls

- One-on-ones, two-on-ones

MEETING SEQUENCE:

■ Two-on-one or one-on-one

■ Small meeting or home meeting

■ Hotel meeting

■ Large hotel open meeting

■ Major rallies, conventions and events

Use open meetings for a second look at the program only.

Required Audio Set:
Million Dollar Meetings; The Secrets of Exponential Growth by Tim Sales & Randy Gage.

MEETING STAFF:

- Presenter(s)

- Lobby greeters

- Sign-in table

- Sergeant-at-arms

- Sound person

- Setup people

  - Displays

  - Banners

- Refreshments (if provided)

- Set for 70 percent of expected turnout

- Have product/prosperity display

- Tuesday or Thursday evenings are best

- Put stage at the front of the room

COPY THIS CHECKLIST AND USE FOR EACH MEETING:

☐ Thermostat set at 65 degrees (one hour before meeting)

☐ All audio-visual equipment tested

☐ Display tables set up

☐ Pre-meeting music ready (45 minutes before meeting)

☐ Tape cued for end-of-meeting music

☐ Name tags ready

☐ Registration table with sign-in sheet (no phone number or address) set up

☐ Meeting posted in the lobby

☐ Proper lighting tested and ready

☐ Company banners, posters, etc., in place

☐ Microphone and volume level checked

☐ Literature packets for guests prepared

☐ Product demonstration area set up (if applicable)

☐ Tickets on hand

☐ Door prizes on hand

☐ Recognition awards on hand

MEETING ETIQUETTE:

■ Wear proper attire.

■ Be on time.

■ Remember, no food, gum, etc.

■ Be generous with applause and laughter.

■ Participate!

■ Introduce guests around.

■ Sit up front.

Notes:

Notes:

Notes:

Notes:

The Follow-Through Process

THE RATIO:

Prospecting 25%

Making Presentations............................25%

Follow-Up and Follow-Through 50%

OFFER THE
3 ALTERNATIVES:

1. Small Business

- Buy wholesale
- Market to friends, neighbors and relatives

2. Big Business

- Lifetime residual income
- Buy wholesale
- Retail profits

3. Shop-At-Home Service

- Save $
- Quality products
- Guaranteed
- Home delivery

■ Bring the necessary materials to every meeting (company materials, packets, follow-up packets, etc.).

■ Always have pre-approach packets available to you.

■ Pull out your calendar as soon as you give out a packet.

■ If you cannot follow-up within 48 hours, don't make a presentation.

■ Keep your posture!

NEW DISTRIBUTORS:

■ 2 meetings the first week,
        then
1 night a week <u>only</u>!

#1 Obligation

```
┌─────────────────────────────────────────┐
│                                          │
└─────────────────────────────────────────┘
```

#2 Obligation

```
┌─────────────────────────────────────────┐
│                                          │
└─────────────────────────────────────────┘
```

■ Your new distributor will lose respect for you if she is most of your organization.

■ Never do more than is necessary.

■ Duplicate yourself.

NEW DISTRIBUTORS:

■ Invest 5-7 meetings to see if you have a builder.

■ Look for core qualities.

■ When you find a 2- to 4-year plan-builder, edify the sponsorship line and send them up.

■ Build a builder past $5,000 per year break-even (self-development materials, functions).

MYTH:

The products don't really matter. As long as the compensation plan is lucrative, that will drive the opportunity.

FACT:

If people don't see real value in the products — they will not continue to order them. Strong network marketing organizations are built on strong products.

DOES THIS HAPPEN TO YOU?

When you make presentations to people who don't want to build a business, how often do they:

◼ Sign up to buy the products wholesale?

◼ Inquire about buying retail?

If this is not happening, look at:

◼ Are you emphasizing "hype" and "rah-rah" tactics?

◼ Are you giving enough attention to the products in your presentation?

◼ Do your products have perceived value with the general public?

Do You Have to Sell?

Can you be your own best customer? ☐

Can you sell products at wholesale costs? ☐

Can you sell below wholesale cost? ☐

Most volume in MLM companies is produced by personal consumption and products which are ☐ ☐

to friends, neighbors and relatives. Non-sales can build organizations that produce sales volumes of hundreds of thousands of dollars.

Crucial Point:
Product must be getting to the

☐ ☐.

Inventories:

■ No need for large stockpiles of products.

■ Sign up direct customers.

■ Make sure you have enough to start new distributors and customers.

Reasons to Develop a Consumer Group:

1. [ ]
2. [ ]
3. [ ]
4. [ ]
5. [ ]
6. [ ]

Don't Pre-judge:

Get your consumers from the people who disqualify themselves from being business-builders.

Notes:

Notes:

Notes:

Building Depth

CORE QUALITIES OF EFFECTIVE ORGANIZATIONAL GROWTH:

■ Laying foundation for the system

■ Insuring duplication

■ Developing infrastructure

■ Going to the next level from recruiting to teaching

■ Developing leaders in the organization

CORE QUALITIES OF A KEY PLAYER:

1. Makes regular presentations

2. Develops a customer base

3. A 100% user of the products

4. Sets aside daily self-development time

5. Attends everything

6. Teachable

7. Accountable

8. Edifies sponsorship

9. Follows the system

Notes:

Notes:

Notes:

Notes:

Using Tools to Build Faster

ARE YOU A BUSINESS-BUILDER?

If so, you'll need some tools.

Tools help your business. They keep you duplicatable and help you withstand the negative forces that will tear it down:

■ Apathy

■ Overly zealous regulators

■ Skepticism

If you don't invest in your business, no one else will.

Don't work with people who won't invest in tools to build their business.

If they aren't willing to invest in tools, you shouldn't be willing to invest your time in training them!

If the people show some initiative, work with them in helping them buy tools. If they can't afford the tools, but are willing to sacrifice a little time and effort in getting them, work with them.

The single most important tool is a

_____.

Don't waste time with people who don't use one!

RECOMMENDED RESOURCES:

Pre-Approach Items

■ **Lifestyle Freedom Pack***
(*Money for Life* Special Report and *Escape the Rat Race* audiotape in specially-designed album).

Alternate Choices

■ **Tapes**
- *"Escape the Rat Race*"*
- *"Future Choice/Rat Race Audio Album"**

■ **Booklets**
- *"Money, Money, Money, Money, Money"**
- *"Money for Life"* Special Report*

■ **Books**
- *"Your Destiny: Your Life & Work Become One"**
- *"Future Choice: Why Network Marketing May Be Your Best Career Choice"**

RECOMMENDED RESOURCES:

Get Started Packet
(When A Distributor Sponsors In)

- ■ *"What You Need to Know First,"* Tape* — Gage

- ■ *"Get Started"* Tape* – Gage

- ■ *"Greatest Networker in the World,"* Book* — Fogg

- ■ *"Secrets of a Dynamic Day,"* Tape* — Gage

- ■ *"Big Al Tells All,"* Book* — Schreiter

Company Materials Packet

- ■ *"Your Destiny: Your Life & Work Become One,"* Book* — Natiuk

- ■ *"Future Choice: Why Network Marketing May Be Your Best Career Move,"* Book* — Anderson/Clouse

- ■ *"Future Choice / Rat Race,"* Tape Album* — Anderson/Clouse

- ■ *"Great Health Thru Nutrition,"* Tape (for nutritional programs)* — Gage

RECOMMENDED RESOURCES:

Developmental Training

■ *"How to Build a Multi-Level Money Machine; The Science of Network Marketing"* Book* — Gage

■ *"Turbo MLM,"* Book* — Schreiter

■ *"Super Prospecting: Special Offers & Quick-Start Systems"* Book* — Schreiter

■ *"How To Earn At Least $100,000 A Year In Network Marketing,"** — Gage

■ *"Business Builder MLM Day Planner Action Pack with mlm tax diary"** — Network Action Company

Web Sites

www.NetworkMarketingTimes.com

www.mlm-metro.com

www.GageDirect.com

Get your free MLM Special Report **Success in Direct Selling**, featuring Randy Gage online or by calling 1-800-946-7804 or 316-942-1111.

RECOMMENDED RESOURCES:

Maintaining Motivation & Focus

■ *"Dynamic Development Series,"** — Gage

■ *"Book-Of-The-Month Program"*

■ *"Weekly/Monthly Tape Program"*

■ *"Upline"*

■ *"The Network Trainer"*

Marketing

■ *"Cash Copy,"* Book* — Lant

■ *"Million Dollar Mailbox"* Binder* — Gage

■ *"Magic Words That Bring You Riches,"* Book — Nicholas

■ *"The 22 Immutable Laws of Marketing,"* Book — Ries/Trout

■ *"Positioning,"* Book — Ries/Trout

■ *"Copywriter,"* Book — Caples

■ *"Scientific Advertising,"* Book — Hopkins

* Available from Prime Concepts Group
1-800-946-7804 or (316) 942-1111
www.NetworkMarketingTimes.com

Notes:

Notes:

Notes:

Building Big $$$ Long Distance

THE BEST KEPT SECRET IN NETWORK MARKETING

Your [   ] lines are
your [   ] [   ] ones!

Long distance sponsorship diversifies and protects your income.

"Extra width brings you income...

Extra depth brings you security...

Long distance sponsoring brings you both."

–R.G.

REASONS TO SPONSOR LONG DISTANCE:

■

■

■

■

■

■

DRAWBACKS:

■

■

EXPENSIVE VS. INVESTMENT:

- Use the tools.

- Use phone, fax, mail and delivery services.

- Make three-way calls, conference calls and demand conferences.

- Follow the same system long distance as you do locally!

WHEN YOU TRAVEL:

- Build a beachhead first.

- Have local leaders participate.

- Stay all weekend.

- Conduct opportunity meetings, training and get-started meetings.

- Follow up when you get home.

DO LOCAL DURING THE WEEK — LONG DISTANCE ON WEEKENDS.

Notes:

Notes:

Notes:

Advanced Leadership Strategies

THE #1 REASON PEOPLE FAIL IN NETWORK MARKETING...

They fail to [   ] and

[   ] with their

[   ].

Your sponsorship line is your best source of help. Keep going up until you find someone who needs the security of depth. Find out how he or she communicates (calls and/or voicemail, after meetings), then replicate through your organization.

Don't be at cross-purpose with your sponsor. If you are, you are the problem.

MONTHLY COUNSELING

■ Do it once a month.

■ Front line or key players.

■ It's best right after the printout is available.

■ Counseling gives you a progress report so you can:

- Note problem areas;
- Make plans;
- Identify leaders; and,
- Take immediate corrective action when necessary.

ORGANIZATION PROGRESS REPORT

Name ..... [   ]

Month..... [   ]

Rank ..... [   ]

# of Distributors .... [   ]

# of Lines .... [   ]

Average Volume .... [   ]

# of Distributorships at Last Function ...... [   ]

# of Lines at Last Function .... [   ]

Personal Use Volume .... [   ]

Total Personal Volume .... [   ]

Group Volume .... [   ]

# of Presentations Made .... [   ]

# of Active Personal Enrollees .... [   ]

# of Inactive Personal Enrollees .... [   ]

# of Distributors Who Did Exact
    Minimum Volume Necessary to Qualify ... [   ]

# of Lines with a Leader .... [   ]

Total # of Leaders in the Organization ...... [   ]

Draw out organization on back.

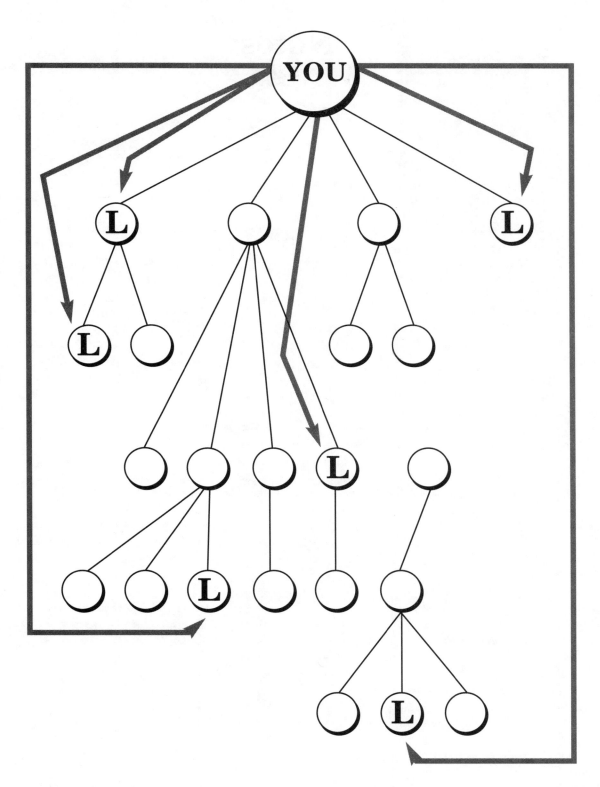

Work with the lowest level leader in a line!

Notes:

Notes:

Notes:

Building a Better You

"We attract into our lives the people and circumstances which are in alignment with the energy signals we emit. If we emit signals of anger, we attract people and circumstances that bring anger into our lives. If we emit signals of happiness, we attract people and circumstances that bring happiness into our lives. It's that simple and it works that way, all the time — with no exceptions."

— Arnold Patent
Excerpted from, *"You Can Have It All"*

"To create a dynamic, growing network — become a dynamic, growing person."

–R.G.

"Your network will grow only as fast as you do."

–Randy Gage

Notes:

Notes:

Answer Key

SECTION 10
Page 10-1   Strongest, long distance
Page 10-2   Over-zealous Attorney Generals, negative publicity, economic
conditions, losing key people, natural disasters, travel & tax advantages
Can't always be there
Cost

SECTION 11
Page 11-1   Identify, work, leaders

To get additional copies of this Study Guide and other business-building resources contact the person with whom you got this Study Guide from or contact:

Prime Concepts Group, Inc.
1807 S. Eisenhower St.
Wichita, KS 67209-2810 USA
1-800-432-4243 or 316-942-1111
www.NetworkMarketingTimes.com

About the Author

Randy Gage is regarded by many as the preeminent expert on Network Marketing in the world today. Tens of thousands of people around the globe credit Randy with helping them reach higher levels of success. For more than 15 years, Randy has been helping people in the direct selling industry break through self-limiting beliefs and achieve their dreams.

Rather than "rah-rah" hype, Randy focuses on specific, how-to training you can use to build your business faster. He has emerged as the highest paid, most sought-after speaker and consultant in the industry. His *How to Earn at Least $100,000 a Year in Network Marketing* audiotape series is the #1 selling album in network marketing history. Randy has conducted training in almost all the fifty United States and in many other countries around the world.

Born in 1959 in Madison, Wisconsin, Randy now lives in Miami Beach, Florida. His hobbies include car racing, baseball and collecting comic books.

For more information about Randy Gage visit his official web site at www.GageDirect.com